DISNEY
CLUB PENGUIN

WADDLE ON!

SUNBIRD

Published by Ladybird Books Ltd 2011
A Penguin Company

Penguin Books Ltd, 80 Strand,
London, WC2R 0RL, UK
Penguin Books Australia Ltd,
Camberwell, Victoria, Australia
Penguin Group (NZ), 67 Apollo Drive, Rosedale,
Aukland 0632, New Zealand
(a division of Pearson New Zealand Ltd)

www.ladybird.com

ISBN: 9781409390824
Printed in China
001 - 10 9 8 7 6 5 4 3 2 1

WADDLE ON!

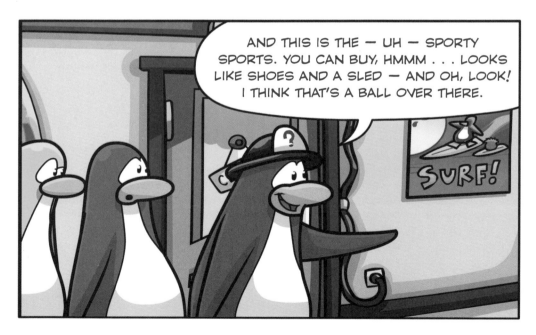

5-DAY FORECAST

THURSDAY	
FRIDAY	
SATURDAY	
SUNDAY	
MONDAY	

AROUND CLUB PENGUIN

HMM, I WONDER WHAT WOULD HAPPEN IF I TURNED IT BY FLIPPER INSTEAD OF SNOWBALLS.

POP!

TRIP!

PUFFLES, PUFFLES, PUFFLES

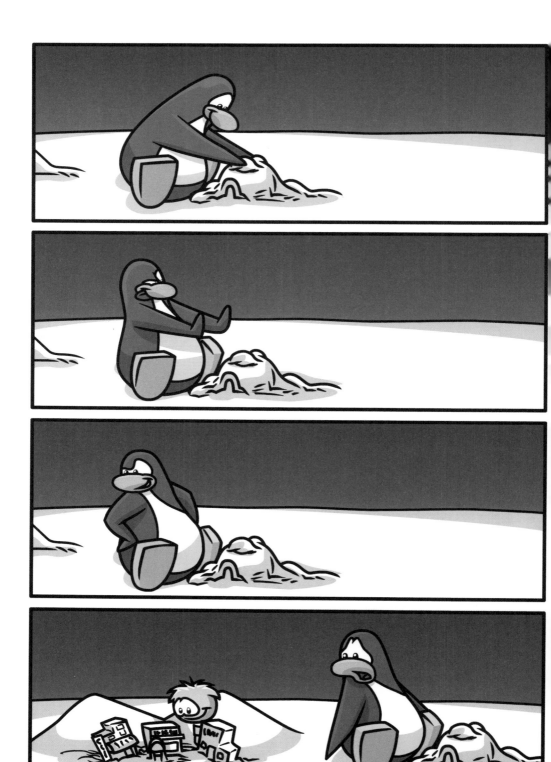

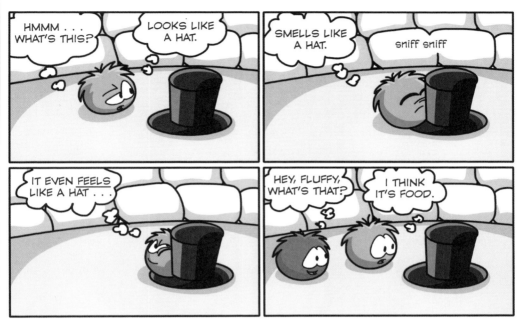

FAMOUS FRIENDS

SKI LIFT 1000

TOASTER 1000

KABOOM

ORANGE JUICE 1000

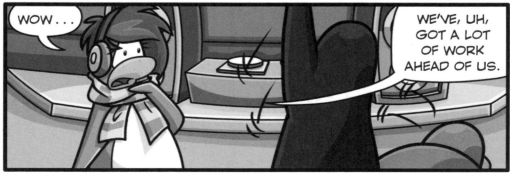

ALL FUN AND GAMES

WHY ARE YOU EVEN _DOING_ THAT?

HUH.

I NEVER THOUGHT ABOUT **WHY** WE THROW SNOWBALLS.

WE JUST DO!

Paf!

BOOSH! WATER BEATS FIRE!

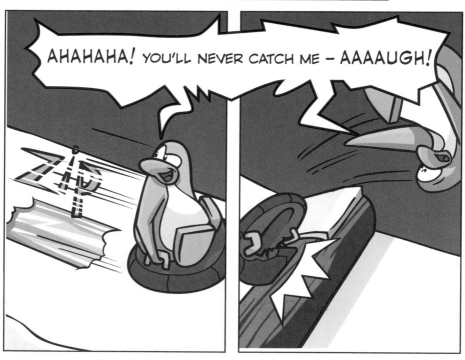

WEEEE!

FLUMP!.

STUPID LOG!

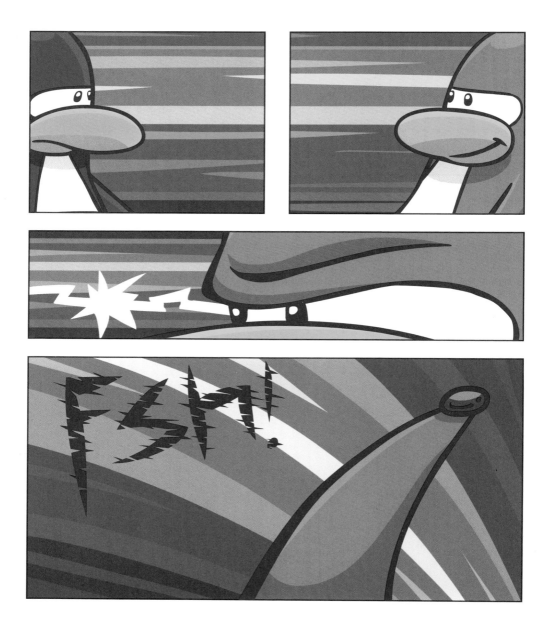

X-TREME JETPACK SURFCARTZ

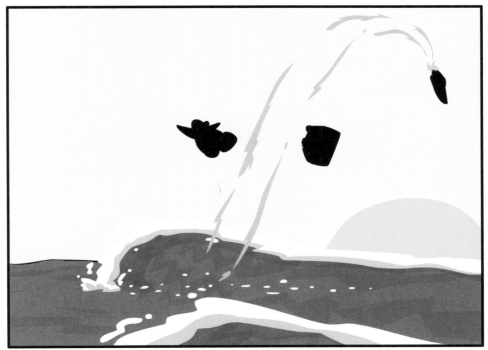